Teachers
Community Workers

by Alice K. Flanagan

Content Adviser: Darryl Figuero,
Senior Professional Associate, Communications Department,
National Education Association

Reading Adviser: Dr. Linda D. Labbo,
College of Education, Department of Reading Education,
The University of Georgia

COMPASS POINT BOOKS

Minneapolis, Minnesota

Compass Point Books
3722 West 50th Street, #115
Minneapolis, MN 55410

Visit Compass Point Books on the Internet at *www.compasspointbooks.com* or e-mail your
request to *custserv@compasspointbooks.com*

Photographs ©:
International Stock/Scott Barrow, cover; PhotoDisc, 4; Unicorn Stock Photos/Bachmann, 5; James L. Shaffer, 6, 7,
10, 11, 17, 21; Unicorn Stock Photos/Rich Baker, 8; Bud Titlow/Visuals Unlimited, 9; Unicorn Stock Photos/Chuck
Schmeiser, 12; Unicorn Stock Photos/Dennis MacDonald, 16, 18; Photo Network/Jeffrey W. Myers, 15; Nancy
Alexander/Visuals Unlimited, 14; Jeff Greenberg/Visuals Unlimited, 19; Sally VanderLaan/Visuals Unlimited, 20;
Photri-Microstock/David Lissy, 22; Unicorn Stock Photos/Jeff Greenberg, 23; Eric Anderson/Visuals Unlimited, 25;
Photri-Microstock, 26; Photo Network, 27.

Editors: E. Russell Primm and Emily J. Dolbear
Photo Researcher: Svetlana Zhurkina
Photo Selector: Linda S. Koutris
Designer: Bradfordesign, Inc.

Library of Congress Cataloging-in-Publication Data

Flanagan, Alice K.
   Teachers / by Alice K. Flanagan.
     p. cm. — (Community workers)
   ISBN 0-7565-0066-4
   1. Teachers—United States—Juvenile literature. [1. Teachers. 2. Occupations.] I. Title. II. Series.
   LB1775.2 .F63 2001
   371.1'00973—dc   21 00-011719

Table of Contents

What Do Teachers Do?

Teachers help people learn. Most of the teachers you know work in schools. They teach reading, mathematics, and science. They also teach foreign languages, art, and music. Some teachers teach many things, or **subjects**. Others teach students only one subject.

This teacher explains an arithmetic problem.

Teachers help people learn new things.

Teachers can help children and adults learn. Some teachers teach a special skill, such as using a computer or driving a truck. And some teachers teach others how to teach!

Some teachers work with adults.

Many teachers help students learn computer skills.

Where Do They Work?

Most teachers work in elementary schools, middle schools, high schools, and colleges. They work in public or private schools. Sometimes they take students on **field trips**.

Most teachers also work at home. At night, they grade papers and prepare **lesson plans** for the next day.

A teacher and his students take a field trip.

A teacher shows his students some of the mysteries of the world.

Who Do They Work With?

Teachers work with the principal. The principal is the person who runs the school. Teachers also work with the school secretary, the librarian, **custodians**, and other teachers. Of course, teachers work with their students most of the time.

◀ A teacher works with other teachers.

A school principal ▶ talks with an elementary schoolteacher.

What Training Does It Take?

All teachers must graduate from college. They learn about the subject they will teach. Then they do their **student teaching**. They learn to follow a teaching plan called a **curriculum**. After they pass a test to teach in their state, they get a **teaching certificate**. This certificate names the grades and subjects they may teach.

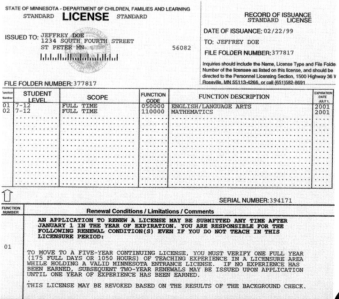

All teachers must go to college.

A teaching certificate

What Skills Do Teachers Need?

Teachers need good speaking skills. They talk to people all day long. They need good reading and writing skills too. Good teachers know about many things and enjoy learning.

A teacher reads to her class.

Teachers must help students learn for themselves.

Being a teacher is a big job. It can be hard to teach students with different needs. Teachers must be patient and well organized. They also should be able to make subjects interesting. Having lots of energy helps too!

A teacher works with a student on a science project.

Teachers help make learning interesting.

What Tools and Equipment Do They Use?

Teachers use all kinds of things to help people learn. They use books, charts, and maps. They write on chalkboards. They use **audiovisual equipment** to show films. Science teachers use microscopes and **Bunsen burners**. Today's teachers use computers and the Internet.

◄ Teachers use maps to help students learn about the world.

Computers can be useful in the classroom. ►

What Problems Do They Face?

Some teachers have too many students in their classes. Not all of the children behave well. Some teachers do not get the help they need from parents. Sometimes teachers do not have supplies. They spend their own money to buy the things they need.

◀ Sometimes teachers shop for their own classroom supplies.

Teachers help students learn how to get along. ▶

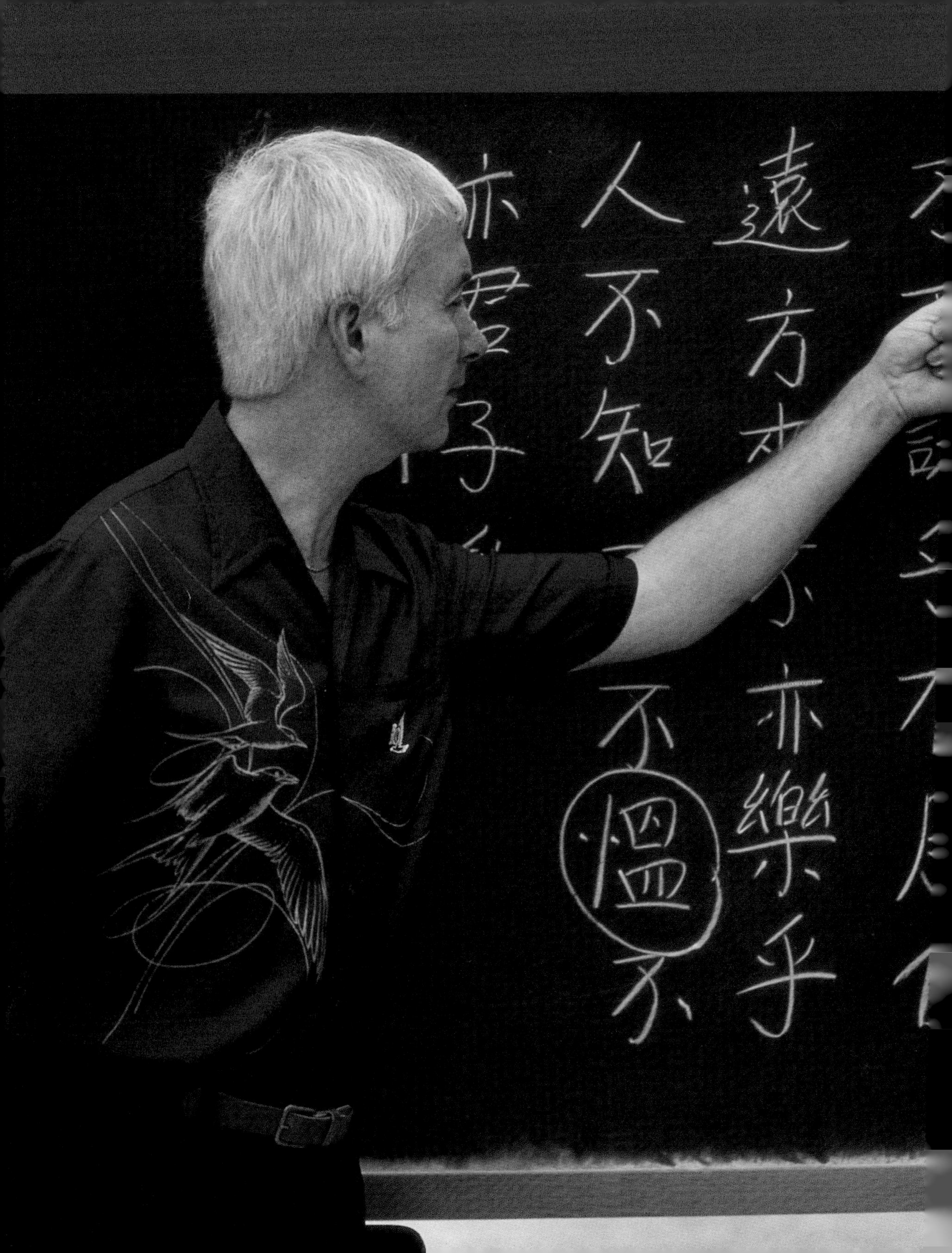

How Do Teachers Help?

Without teachers and schools, we would not know much about our world. Most people would not know how to read or write. Some people could not get jobs. Teachers help us learn what we need to know. They make our community a better place to live.

◄ This teacher is helping adults learn Chinese.

Some teachers ► teach students with special needs.

Would You Like to Be a Teacher?

Do you like to help others learn new things? Maybe you would like to be a teacher someday. You can prepare now. At home, help your brother or sister with homework. Teach a friend how to do something. In school, do your best in every subject. Be a good student. Help your teacher. And help others to learn.

◀ Helping a younger brother or sister is a good way to explore being a teacher.

These two girls ▶ are playing school at home.

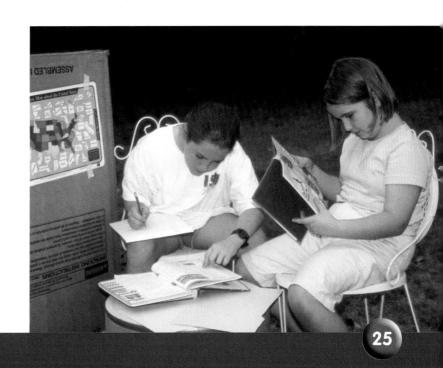

A Teacher's Tools

chalkboard

textbook

In the Classroom

poster

chalkboard

pointer

desk

eraser

A Teacher's Day

Morning
- The teacher arrives at school early. He organizes his desk and reads the newspaper.
- He greets his students and takes attendance.
- In the first lesson of the day, the teacher asks students to read aloud from their social studies textbooks.
- After break, the teacher gives a short math test. Then he explains new arithmetic problems on the blackboard.

Noon
- The teacher eats his lunch in the teacher's lounge. He talks with other teachers about the new computers in the school library.

Afternoon
- The teacher listens as the students give reports about books they have read.
- Then he shows the class a film about polar bears.
- The teacher assigns homework for tomorrow.
- After school is over, the teacher holds tryouts for the school play.

Evening
- After dinner with his family, the teacher grades math tests.
- Then he prepares lessons for the next day.

Glossary

audiovisual equipment—machines that use sound and pictures to teach things

Bunsen burners—small gas burners used in science experiments

curriculum—a plan for what students should study

custodians—people who clean and take care of school buildings

field trips—visits with a group to see things and learn

lesson plans—ideas about how to teach specific skills and information

student teaching—practice teaching with the help of an experienced teacher

subjects—areas of study, such as science or mathematics

teaching certificate—an official paper that names the grades and subjects a person may teach

Did You Know?

- Long ago, classes with students of all ages were held in one-room schoolhouses.

- There are almost 50 million teachers in the world.

- The United States has about 3 million teachers in elementary and high schools.

- The oldest public school in the United States is the Boston Latin School in Massachusetts. It opened in 1635.

Want to Know More?

At the Library

Deedrick, Tami. *Teachers.* Mankato, Minn.: Bridgestone Books, 1998.

Greene, Carol. *Teachers Help Us Learn.* Chanhassen, Minn.: The Child's World, 1997.

Lehn, Barbara. *What Is a Teacher?* Brookfield, Conn.: Millbrook Press, 2000.

Schomp, Virginia. *If You Were a Teacher.* Tarrytown, N.Y.: Benchmark Books, 2000.

On the Web

Teachers Helping Teachers

http://www.pacificnet.net/~mandel/

For advice, tips, and lesson plans

Teachers.Net

http://teachers.net/

For resources for teachers

Through the Mail

American Federation of Teachers

555 New Jersey Avenue, N.W.

Washington, DC 20001

To get information about teaching

On the Road

University of Pennsylvania

235 South 33rd Street

Philadelphia, PA 19104

215/243-9880

To tour one of the country's most historic colleges

Index

About the Author

Alice K. Flanagan writes books for children and teachers. Since she was a young girl, she has enjoyed writing. She has written more than seventy books on a wide variety of topics. Some of her books include biographies of U.S. presidents and their wives, biographies of people working in our neighborhoods, phonics books for beginning readers, and informational books about birds and Native Americans. Alice K. Flanagan lives in Chicago, Illinois.